THE MAFIA ACCORDING
TO TERESA DI SCLAFANI

TERESA DI SCLAFANI DE NASCA

CONTENTS

1. The Mafia   1
2. The Bandit 1900 - 1950   13
3. Contaminated Policy   19
4. The cholera of 1837 and 1867   21
5. Illustrious Man   23
6. Lieutenant Cutrona   25
7. Professor Giovanni Salemi   27
8. Captain Medical Doctor Damiano Drago   29
9. Coronel Doctor Emilio Militello   33
10. Monsignor Doctor Rafaele Arrigo   35
11. Montemaggiore Medallions   37
12. Professor Medical Doctor Captain Giuseppe Mendola   39
13. Professor Francesco Biondolillo   41
14. Doctor Professor Pietro Drago   43
15. Priest Lawyer Emilio Drago   47
16. Monsignor Doctor Liborio Scaccia   49
17. The Offender's Children   53
   (historical romance)
18. Newspapers and books   63

About the Author   65
More works by Teresa Di Sclafani De Nasca   67

THE MAFIA ACCORDING TO TERESA DI SCLAFANI

ISBN of the printed paperback version:

979-8-9909036-6-1

ISBN of the electronic version (*ebook*):

979-8-9909036-7-8

1

THE MAFIA

Ortolero died in prison and Carlino the same. Seven were sentenced to life imprisonment, others to 30 years and others to 130 years in prison, according to the Sicilian newspaper:

- October 1, 1927
- October 11, 1927
- 7 February 1928
- June 27, 1929
- 21 February 1930
- June 7, 1931

Commander Mori captured Rafalo Carlino's gang in Sciacca in an eight-hour operation. The mafioso Grisali had been transferred to the mainland to fight crime in Sicily. He was a politician, prefect of Palermo.

In his speech of June 6, 1926, Mori spoke about Sicily's last bandit and the social duty in tax collection. He said that Sicily eliminated a piece of scum, Spinelo Perticone.

An article in an Italian newspaper of July 21, 1931 noted that Sicily ranked first in Mafia-related crime.

Lucio Drago Saleme was a bandit from Sicily. At that time, the Mafia controlled the governments of the day and the magistrates of the neighboring countries, who called themselves «galandomini» of justice.

His Catholic Majesty Philip V of Spain conquered freedom with the Mafia, but the Sicilians rose up against the Bourbon and all the Italians turned against him on January 12, 1848.

In Palermo on April 4, 1860, the bells rang with the arrival of Giuseppe Garibaldi to the movement that united Sicily in defense of freedom, law and morality. He did not count on the fact that all obeyed Bourbon and in 1861 he sent the lord of Calabria. Angelo Pugliese joins Cicero Guccione of Alia. In San Giovanni, Don Pepino Il Lombardo hid four mafiosios in Lercara.

A young knight on a white horse appeared and met three respectable gentlemen. Don Pepino accepted the visit, but two young carabineros were surprised by a group of 50 delinquents, who turned them into gunpowder.

A young Neapolitan man named Marcos, who had killed his own father, carried several amulets and had promised the Virgin of the Chain to share his strength. In Salemi, many people united to defend themselves against the Mafia. Lombardo's gang wreaked havoc and disappeared.

The gangsters were the soul of Don Pepino. Fearful for their families, they join the feared Lombardo. On the last day of April, the most feared of the bandits is transported by boat with political aid. The bandits were condemned on November 25.

While Lombardo is in Africa, they pass in front of a building of the Italian vice-consul. They were arrested by five Turkish policemen and taken to the provincial jail, under the supervision of the Assisi court. On May 28, 1868 another Mafioso was beheaded, condemned by Pugliese after the revolt of August 20, 1860.

Biagio Valvo was the ringleader. The Mafia begins and ends with the minister. The lords of the government of the day, between 1860 and 1870, were related to the Mafia including a captain. They had horses, guns and ammunition. They were always well dressed and looked like government lords.

In a speech on June 11, 1875, the government was asked to recognize its errors. It sent General Medici, armed with ammunition and weapons, to restore confidence in justice. The procurator general Nicotera was a fake, with Mafia links in Palermo and other cities east of Palermo, Sicily, Florence and Rome. Using Mafia officials, he sends a message to the lieutenant and informs him about a clandestine wine stash.

The lieutenant, who is close to Guccione, looks for them everywhere and does not find them, because they were in the winter house. They stabbed a notary and two years later, in 1869, the notary repeats the game to the mafioso. He joins the public security guard.

A woman reports that stolen objects are found in the palace of the Marchioness and Countess Tasca, and Sebastiano Giotti, a public security guard, discovers all the stolen items.

The prefect of Palermo decides to call Guccione, a man of character, to assume the position of military commander, in charge of a hunt to apprehend 25,000 a year. However, Guccione does not accept the position. He calls him back and says: «Commander, I have come to resign.» Surprised, he realizes that his conversation with the prefect was a prefectural secret.

They threw a carnival ball with masks, where all the bandits were there with the owners of the houses. One day he said he wanted to meet the famous bandit and a month later, the baron of Caltanissetta introduced them.

All happy, walking in the streets of Palermo, attending the theater and the best restaurants, with the son of the murderer Valvo. The prefect suggests to the bandit that, if he wishes to travel, he should do so under a false name.

One day, Valvo had bad teeth. He was in the Raciura fief of Alia, smoking, dancing and getting impatient, talking about all the bad things that Valvo and the band leader were doing. They changed residence on June 7, 1873.

At the end, Brigadier Bonomo and three clerks were by Mercatobianco. When they arrived at the house, they saw the bandits. Valvo was alone and a brief combat begins. A rifle shot wounds the horse in the eye. A military man throws a rifle shot and shot himself, dying.

Valvo sleeps under the trees and is awakened by the passing of the horse. He threw a blow, but he was already dead and falls to the ground. Another shot is fired by the soldier, a blow to the squad. The band leader, badly wounded, wields the pistol and says, «You have me dead.». Being alive was never the fault Valvo shot themselves.

And if they already jumped the brain at the end of the famous and so feared, has made history the dead Sicilian bandit, Valvo «The Fierce One». Di Pasquale and Leone prepared the revenge against the brigadier Bonomo in Valvo's house, on September 14, 1873. They made a meeting with big Mafiosi: Di Pasquale, Leone, Salpietro and Di Carlo, with the Mafia of Montemaggiore, Alia and several villages. It was in a big restaurant, where 50 mafiosi ate.

On the 21st of the same month, Bonomo was talking to two blond military men near the house. Riding with two horses from Calvario, they came to the village. He met Brigadier Natale and loving company, with the weapons of Mr. Saeli, soon recognized mafioso of Cefalù.

Although during the Easter vacations, in April 1875, they were going to eliminate the sweet nest of lieutenant Domenico Ilardi, it fell into the hands of the public forces and the Leone gang, mortified by the loss of its leader, was left without a champion.

Paulino Di Carlo was found dead in the Cardollino fief. It was said that it was the end of poverty. Di Pasquale and Leone were rivals who were in my propaganda in the last century. Modern Mafia, generosity and chivalry remain in the darkness of crime, in the bank and in the blood. In the criminal world of the Mafia there is no gesture of generosity or chivalry.

Labor was destroyed by the Mafia. Weapons permits were given to honest people and they were not given power or wealth.

Musolino was a mafioso of category, Calabrian and military. They made with 500 carabinieri and 500 delegates, but it was 2 carabinieri who were caught like a fox in a trap. The bandit Musolino was then tried in Tuscany and then incarcerated in the Catanzaro prison.

After 3 years, for few thousand liras, for fierce of any court of Assisi, they did not have the application of the penal code. The convict had committed 90 homicides and 14 unsuccessful homicides. 1500 that could be in favor of Sicily, giving him some railroads. It said that it was charity blood, that it shoots treacherously in the process of 1902.

They did not feel horror, but contempt for the migrants because of their laziness to return to Italy. I wanted to see the mafias I did not know. The newspapers of Milan, Turin and Genoa, saying the new aqueduct and southern, the poor heroes of the south, was of evil curiosity to know.

Pasquali writes a postcard to his friend, saying goodbye to Musolino, a victim of nature. Musolino in hiding lived thinking of spiritual existence. There was a lot of political and moral disorder.

Giuseppe Balamani was an occasional bandit. After staying in the mountain among the ruins, he is caught by the P.S., the Assisi Court of Perugia. The murderer of Giordano the Salamon is in prison. His self-defense presents a known victim of Giordano, his girlfriend Bonincontro. He remembers his mother. What Salamon tells has a meaning and he ends up voting, victim of crime, to procure the welfare and happiness of Giordano the Salamon. He was murdered and sentenced to life imprisonment.

F. P. Varsalone was the leader of bandits, at the point of terror and death, in Agrigento, Caltanisetta and Bivona. A shepherd of Castrenovo makes extortions and revenge, who as a boy lived in misery. He wields weapons and the bird of the forest, son of bandits. His father is a friend of Pepino Il Lombardo. He was arrested and killed in prison.

The father took on the crime with the cold-bloodedness of the Varsalone family. The young men, four brothers, died in prison. The race, a multiple crime in 1892. They were close to many institutions that were placed under his protection.

Varsalone took command and got close to the head of the Palermo Mafia, old Carlino. But Varsalone was not second-rate. Carlino's gang, from Cesaro's boat, operated valiantly.

Brother Lanza is imprisoned in the territory of Cefalù. Two rival chiefs end the conflicts between Carlino, who only seeks an agreement with Varsalona. The agreement included the condition to kill the father in prison, reflecting the instinct of the crime and the moral character of the sons and brothers who were killed in prison. The race was inaugurated in 1892.

Leonardo Provenzano was close to his directors. Varsalone took command and turned to Carlino as gang leader on the Palermo side. The Lanza brothers of Cefalù, now with Carlino and Varsalone, were mafiosi who divided the territories of the provinces: Caccamo, Cerda, Caltanissetta, Sclafani, Valledolmo, with Varsalone, with the comrades Brunogolfo and Guzino in 1893.

The gang respects Coletti Runbola, who was found dead three months later in Mangiapane Michelangelo's house. His son is kidnapped and he goes to the authorities. Varsalone claims to be a foreigner. He kidnaps and frees the kidnapped, making the family pay little. The ingenious Mangiapane has little money and thanks Varsalone, in front of his wife, daughter and mother.

Mangiapane is overwhelmed with shame. He protests and defends Tinito Vitale of Castrenovo, who suspects that Varsalone wants to seduce his wife, Maria Barbarino. He is led to love kindness.

La Chirezza Vicenza, one of the Varsalone girls, was found dead together with Tinito in 1897 and they were buried one on top of the other. Many fell with this gang: Panepinto

Pasquale, the comrade P. S. Guardia of Valledolmo, and others like Gamelia, the boar Tringaid, and Poliler.

Montemaggiore's father, leader of the Varsalone gang, was linked to the crime of Gennaura of Alia and Morreale of the caves. The new members of the gang are unaware of the Mafia criminal code, although they know the crimes committed on his initiative and the associate prosecutor B. F. Varsalone, whom he threatens with death.

Subsequently, Dissalfi of Montalbano of Sciara, receives the pardon and delivers it to the knight Alfaro of Sciara. He then threatens Gennauro with Morriale, kidnaps the G. of Alia and asks as condition of Gennauro's father and Varsalone as defender of the G. of Alia.

Gennaro and Morreale are killed and land in Goldfinch and Carpinello. Gennauro's head is thrown to the lions in G. in Alia to welcome this fair act of the Lord of Alia. Varsalone, the first member of the Mafia, is dead but will surely not meet the P.S. in Alia, the fief of the angry Vacco. Varsalone fires shots into the blue sky. In Sicily they speak in hushed tones.

A peasant with improvised wealth is a savage with great capital. Such are the great lords of the time, in and around Alia. Farmers have to know where wealth comes from. Varsalone gets the fief in this way.

El Vacco was walking with Richi Galandomine and was injured in the knee. A doctor from Valledolmo came to treat him. «He came to breathe the air of Belsito, the Palazzo dei

Signori,» he said. The Capobianca missions are governed by the Baron's woods and fiefs, protected by the Palermo authorities.

The criminals were at the Four Corners Hotel. It was a hotel with a restaurant, in the forest of Neuchatel, a hotel of murderers who die like rabbits, where they have frogs, snakes, goats and sheep. The clients are treated very well.

Varsalone's capture was in Sicily. The commissioner Ballante, in agreement with the prefect of Palermo De Seta, the P.S. patrols, looking for the mafioso in the mansions, with closed basements. Simultaneously, they established a reward of 25,000 lire.

Mercadante's wife and young daughter had some experience with gangsters. They gave the girl a scare. In 1904 the Mercadante brothers were men of 30 years in the mafia. Grisanti and Gervasi, landowners of Varsalona, are persecuted in America to get rid of the Mafiosi.

January 3, 1904 marks the 30th anniversary of the P. S.. He was going to Palermo by car when the last letter from the P. S. arrived, warning that they are coming to Italy to hide and look for him.

On December 11, 1934 the Italian newspapers *Virruso* and *Pinello* were detained.

On December 15, 1934, the mob in Andaloro belongs to Perrarello and the entrenched camp of Madonie Carlino and Terrarcillo. Gaetanno suffers from rivalry with the wounded of Perrarello and threatens with a dagger to Doca. The hitman puts a paper in the corpse.

Crazy Gaetano Perrarello decides to retire from the band after reaching an agreement with Carlino. «I lived freely and was a good citizen,» says Borsini. The world is crooked and you have to stay until the end. The command is divided into several groups. Perrarello did not care about the blood flowing from the graves in Andaloro.

The Criminal Court was created in Mistretta, Andaloro, in 1913. Ortolero, one of the biggest in the Mafia, was a lawyer and crime boss. The judges of the court and the King's attorneys were paid by the Mafia.

Di Salvo is a military advisor to Mamma na Pati, Scimeca's brother, and is involved in Ortolero's study operations. They were kidnapped from the island in 1911 by the Mafia of Mistretta, Carlino and Pisciolo Indicello.

The last days of carnival, dressed in a mask, he would advance through the streets of Mistretta, carefully holding his cane. «Viva la Mafia!» («Long live the Mafia!») was his motto as the Moors chased the bandits. He used the public auction bar in the forest as part of his activities.

The powerful of politics, protectors of the Mafia, perfect domicile, bloodless murderers, are brought to justice, collapsed in Madonia. Gaetanno Perrarello faced justice for the first time after 31 years.

2

THE BANDIT 1900 - 1950

L iving in the midst of the Mafia and the military, anyone associated with the Mafia looked at the connections in Montemaggiore Belsito, where the bandits are on the side of society. Thus we find the wife mistreated by her husband. They saw themselves as gentlemen and claimed from the husband the good treatment. Eventually one of these became head of the Mafia.

Women learn and open cafés and restaurants to educate their children, changing their lives and giving strength to the Mafia. They studied a profession, worked outside and sometimes in other towns. The cultural movement, theater and so on.

The whole Mafia was in the sights of the politicians and the military knew who the criminals were. Marshal Geralmi had made a coup to go after the criminals and he was immediately transferred.

The blood crime was washed with blood in the forest of Montemaggiore in 1912. The bad guys seized the animals of the B. Mesi Todaro Salvo and left. The people wanted their animals and the thieves would not give them back. They were insistent, they waited for the return of their animals but they were not returned.

Pace Filippo di Giovanni, whose nickname was Bagella, preferred at the source of Carpinello. The games of Mauro, iron of the band leader Carlino.

On July 26, 1920, the doctor's murderer kills them, a crime in Montemaggiore. The wife of the murdered and the mafioso who travels in the robbery put an end to the investigation. The wife, with the bloody handkerchief, leaves it on his chest as a souvenir.

Judge Di Biaje says to him, «Why do you do it?»

«It is my blood. It has to be avenged.»

Those present were shocked by such a tragic event.

On August 17, 1931 they look for people from outside for the party. Stefano Cirrincione, who was once Rosario de Montemaggiore, approaches them. He threatens him and leaves them 1000 lire. The camp burns. A year later, they got dead Cirrincione Andrea of Rosario, in the fief Gianella. It was a deadly feud, accomplice of Altavilla who had an incurable disease.

The corpse was buried in the woods one autumn afternoon in 1922. Great tragedies are brewing in the Carpinello fief in

Tragara. The Cuggino family of Valledolino lives on the farm, where the two-year-old children offer the prospect of future happiness.

Shot on July 14, 1912, the poor man was riding a horse in the fief of Cacciabar. People dressed as lords killed them. The authorities wanted to act and the P. S. wanted to avenge the dead man. One night, Turillo the Morrealés went to the Magurio forest. He was a man of great skill. He was returning home with his mother when he was surprised and attacked with a gun. None of the neighbors showed up.

In July 1915, the barber Bernardo Messi is threatened by three individuals. They arrived at Calvario and the dealer Pasquale told him to leave. He paid with death.

On January 4, 1918, Todaro Salvatore meets two evildoers and jumps off his horse. Death and the living are the same.

Antonino of Alimiminusa, Filippo di Miguele of Montemaggiore, Castellone of Musulmeli. Many of them were in America and some of them asked forgiveness to the murderer of Pasquale Domenica. On the night of May 1, 1919, 73-year-old Pasquale Domenica and his granddaughter were murdered in their home. A robbery in the house of Di Pasquale, from the office of R. R., several are murdered under the eyes of the authorities.

On June 21, 1920 in the middle of the day, at 9.30 a.m. in Montemaggiore Belsito, the doctor Ignazio Salemi is assassinated with his brother Gaetano. They shot him 5 times and caused his death. It is seen the biggest Mafia of Carpinello and the famous Santangelo, the casino and Bernardo's games.

In a factory house, two bride and groom are having fun in their idyll. They rented to make a party to the entourage to their liking, celebrating the future happiness. An armed band of powerful, the P. S., arrives at the cousin's restaurant. Men, women and children leading the cows, dogs and cats.

The man Castilla Giacomo and Stefano, from Montemaggiore, cause a tragedy with pain. They are the authors of the murder and threaten a victim to blame them. Cristina of Pisa, in power of the fief of Raciura, wanted the dominion of Alia. The Mafia does not allow Cristina to cross Lincoln Street in Palermo. In the end she was blamed for Alia's corpses and crimes.

Bernardo does business at the Roca stations and Palumba is dead. The strength of the horse that was dragging Constanza Giuseppe disappeared. Filomena Guccione of Ferrara well, Caddera Di Gioia, Santo Di Salvo, Antonino Bova, Bernardo Di Piaza, Mariano and his brother Gullo, Tanara Mascarella, S. Russo and La Mendola. They all died for revenge and are the savage heirs of the bandit Giuliano. Something tragic always happens.

Benito Mussolini was preparing the guard and preparing the distractions of Europe. He had imposed great sacrifices on Italy. The Italians could eat 150 grams of bread a day and 50 grams of meat a week. The people were tired from hunger and went to the black market in order to eat.

One day the young Salvatore Giuliano of Montelepre was passing by, carrying a sack of grain. A guard stopped him, arrested him and took the grain from him. Victim of injustice, blood rushes to his head. He arms himself with a bar and a pistol and threatens the carabineros. One dies and the other is seriously wounded, so he flees into hiding.

It is the fate of a village, Montelepre, victim of kidnapping. Giuliano took from the rich and then entered the houses without anyone noticing and left the money. Giuliano made a name for himself in Sicily as a separatist and anti-communist. He hoped that Sicily would have another government, with justice and amnesty.

Colonel Geronazzo of the E.L.V.S. wants to accuse him of a crime and the communists support the carabinieri, but the people support him everywhere. On May 1, 1947, the street had the name of Portella delle Ginestre. It was premeditated when Giuliano ordered to hold fire with blows. There were also Commissar Trappari and Captain Di Salvo.

His band of 150 men was pitted against 80 carabineros, 22 agents and 8 soldiers. The rest were civilians. It ends with 18 bandits dead, 55 wounded and the rest imprisoned. It is believed that Giuliano is the driver of Sicily and that he was thinking of a war for the return to the monarchy and the Mafia.

Colonel Luca, a brave and famous officer in Turkey and England, liberated the area from the gangsters. He accepted the duel because he was suspicious of his friends. On the night of July 5, 1950, Giuliano entered Castelvetrano. Soon after, 500 carabinieri were ordered to confront him. They take Gagini street and a patrol warns of two men coming ahead, they recognize them and capture them.

He manages to hide, immersed in the machine-gun fire. He enters a courtyard where the policeman Barsin was and soon tragedy strikes. The most feared of the Mafia, the biggest bosses of the Sicilian gangs. Such were the episodes of the past. Hopefully we will not return to the republican states, the claims, the protests and the activities allowed by the authority of the Government. The memory of Giuliano will be in the hearts of Sicilians.

It is necessary to read this bitter story as a fable to children, children of bad luck. Thirty years have passed and I knew life, the world, men and how much a citizen is worth.

3

CONTAMINATED POLICY

T hings in 1860 were full of worries and torments, in this people with a political will to death, Capozzi said. The wealth camouflaged as patriotism was a bank of lies, representations of the tragedies of chivalry. Loyalty and colors are exhausted, as well as agents, while things get tragic for the knights.

They were drugstore characters, individuals from another party. Those with own principles of the word, poor people of Dante's light. It was a laboratory with welfare thanks to the thefts of the Mafia and the bad peaceful politics of the citizens. «It was the great wickedness that enriches itself with the poor dispossessed,» says St. Augustine, who walks among those who live and those who die of hunger.

The builder of the Fatherland, Giuseppe Garibaldi, loved agriculture and the sentiment of 1876. He wrote that his profession was agriculture and said that «Beautiful is the man who loves his people.» He was a great French fighter, who loved trees, animals and the great responsibility of the family. He believed that brilliant men in medicine were the most sacred in the political field. If someone wants to deceive the people by believing them ignorant, he would tie them to the side of a conuco.

Everything is premeditated. There is a traditional question and that is that we have to leave this conscience to Montemaggiore, who are the ones who receive the blows. Memories of what is false seduce good people, while farmers work for the welfare of others. Several meaningless blows in Montemaggiore Belsito.

It sends the unknown and drags the honest people to the bad streets. There is a Divine power that searches the bad, the consciences and minds of the false politicians. The people forgive those who do not know what they are doing, but not those who intentionally deceive. The exterior is disappearing, like a shipwreck with no return, culture and wealth also disappear.

Personality, gentleness, energy and love of life mend the heart. Politicians cannot be educated, they tremble and do not repent, and their serious mistakes do great harm to the people and tired humanity. Life was easy, but now wives, children and parents suffer. Political passions and the pursuit of wealth predominate, while few men reason and respect the family.

4

THE CHOLERA OF 1837 AND 1867

In 1837, Montemaggiore suffers from cholera with many fatalities such as Mercurio Teresi, his wife, the King, Filippo Mascarella and the archpriest Giacomo Vasco. In 1867, the epidemic caused more than 70 deaths in a church. In the same house everyone dies: the wife, the brother, the son, the parents, the friend.

The years 1837 and 1867 are of death. The reader is left by unanimous thought with the sigh of nature. The farmer continued his work while the mules fell victim to cholera. The young were the first and it was impossible to count. It affected the solitary, the madman and the consecrations of the churches. It was terrible. The graves were kept as there was no time to bury them. This is the history of cholera and may God take us by surprise.

5

ILLUSTRIOUS MAN

The history of mankind is made up of artists, guerrillas, tyrants, philosophers, liberators, poets of variety, legislators, scientists, great mystics, great criminals. They are little responsible in the face of death and it is up to historians and critics to examine the particular indomitable character of life. The illustrious who influenced machines, two volumes of history and dreams. The words say «burn the letter» and the character with eternal affection. Through the centuries endures the beautiful age.

In Montemaggiore, the illustrious Monsignor Mercurio Maria Teresi, Archbishop of Morriale, was born on October 10, 1742. He was an archpriest renowned for his morals. For three years of his pontificate, our Teresi lived in Morriale. On April 18, 1805, his faithful shed tears for his death, being deeply affected. His remains were taken to Montemaggiore and remain as a precious relic in his temple, noble people who do not forget his precious soul.

In 1926, Professor Di Gesù, custodian and administrator of the cathedral, was at the school in Morriale. He transformed the chapel, renovated the S. S., the crucifix of the cathedral, the two tombs and the relic. During the renovation of the basement of the Arca Teresi, he ordered to close it and not to open it anymore. The presence of the colleague Di Gesù was requested in the illustrious religious sentiment. Monsignor Ruperti took the recommendations to the people.

Di Gesù communicated to H. E. Monsignor Filippi, Archbishop of Morriale, the virtue of Teresi the illustrious. The people of Montemaggiore and its farmers are responsible for the consensus. On the feast of Morriale, came the car accompanying the archpriest, who arrived at the house of the parish priest of the Cathedral, in Salemi. He was an illustrious citizen. The word that the pen writes in the history of Alia is too big for the religious. We are up to date. We have what we donate and the good we do for others.

6

LIEUTENANT CUTRONA

Our Montemaggiore patriots offer their service to the homeland to prevent slavery. We remember Lieutenant Cutrona, who was born on December 27, 1827. He studied at the University of Palermo, obtaining the diploma of Surveyor in 1857. He joined the National Guard in 1848 and became a sergeant of artillery of the A. N. of Sicily, for merit of War.

He fought in several campaigns of the Italian unit and won three medals. The first was bronze, between 1848 and 1849. The second for the liberation of Sicily from southern Italy, in 1860 and 1861. The third for the battle of Compatute, in 1860 to 1866. He was a graduate of Villafranca. General F. Perrinenco praises Cutrona and writes: «Mr. Cutrona Salvatore was the patriotic merit of a good patriot.»

7

PROFESSOR GIOVANNI SALEMI

P rof. Salemi was a historical figure. The intelligent
family of Prof. Giovanni Salemi from Montemaggiore moves to Palermo in 1940. To see the valuable
work of this illustrious fellow citizen, I limit myself to the
Sicilian newspaper up to the day of his death, February 8,
1930. Professor Giovanni Salemi was a noble figure, an illustrious citizen of Palermo and esteemed for his doctrines, his
admirable gifts and his wit.

Salemi was a great citizen, professor emeritus ordinary of
mechanics applied to constructions, with the task of teaching
topography and geography. He was director of the School of
Engineering and member of the Superior Council of Public
Instruction. For years he was president of the College of
Engineering and Architecture. He was advisor to LL. PP.
under the civic administration of Notavartolo and commis-

sioner FF. SS., as well as a member of the 1892 exposition committee.

In the past he was an illustrious activist and appeared with passionate love from the millions of heads and hearts. They made the beloved scientist a salute to the soul revealing the gifts of instinct. Podesta Marchese Maurigi, Greek professor of the engineers' union.

8

CAPTAIN MEDICAL DOCTOR DAMIANO DRAGO

The great men of lofty sentiment on Calvary. God is pleased to call them and accompany them to the grave. Pain and adventure in man to the grave. We are beggars of the earth that embraces man.

Archimedes, condemned to science and killed. Cicero, in Galilee, was martyred. Virgil, outside the homeland he adored, sacrifices himself to free it. Masso was cast adrift in Rome. Columbus dies in chains outside the ruins of Cartagena. Chenier dies at the guillotine in 99, in France. Milton, blind. Beethoven, poor, deaf at the age of 30. In jail, Toscalo, poor and cursed.

Danger in prison and death as a satellite. Sopranos and great men ran with death with courage. Death was untimely, it got its own and did not arrive perfect. Everything implemented was blown away by the wind. Only force rules the world. The religion of Christ that is given at the end of life with pains and justifies death. Jesus of Bethlehem on Golgotha, seeing the blood.

The work code of humanity, the panorama of the other tomb, to all life the pain of Calvary. In front of death are the gratifications of love, greatness is the seal that consecrates fame. Furrowed still by lightning, for the future are we.

Captain Drago was born in Montemaggiore Belsito on October 9, 1901. His father felt the need to leave a memory of the new life and before having children, he spoke to him as a strong young man: «You are going to leave for the war.» Indefatigable in the life to go to a war, look for Cesareo's volume that is well sculpted, that governs the father's spirit when you, with the desire, you will come towards the youth in vague longings.

Suspended I'll be in the cold shadow of death's descent and I'll never see you again. Perhaps the industrial letters I wrote will tell you the dream where I was a prisoner of love, of stories offered by the heart brought in silence. You will not know the life where rising up is a battle, but he who is honored with gentle lineage boldly it behoves him to get there. He goes without battle in weapons of courage, honest but resolute. Here is the path of the young man, engraved in his soul and paternal memory.

At the age of 22, after graduating in medicine and surgery in Palermo, he presents the exams included in the career with the maximum of praise. After the intense life and full of family affection for the good of the fatherland, the young captains doctors, we find them of glorious aurelio. In the young military, the biographer doctor Giovanni Mogavero knew the nature of the character of justice. The greatest intellectual is found in the people of Rome, October 5, 1933. Citizenship followed.

Dad had no strength because of the illness of Captain Damiano Drago, with the pain of death he arrived in Palermo on the night of the 26th. His soul was transported to Montemaggiore by the citizens in a hearse and the pain accompanies the soul. In the Mother Church the following day, the funeral, solemn act of which the people and the authority were participants. In a greeting to the doctor and the authorities, Mogavero Giovani praises the superiors and the heart of instinct.

The lawyer Gaetano Salemi and Giovani Salemi spoke, thanking the citizens for their significant gesture, taking part in the free funeral in honor of Captain Drago. He was a brilliant young man who entered the military health care career in 1924, at the age of 28. He received the rank of Captain Doctor of Italy, for his discipline and duty fulfilled. He is remembered with sorrow, as Montemaggiore lost his prodigal son to a tropical disease.

He was the best of the battalion of officers in the pyroscaff, in charge of the youth and professional community. The Minister of War B. Mussolini gives him the distinction of honor for death in service, dated Rome 23 November 1915, signed by the minister himself and sent by telegram to the family. True armed artillery officers, commander Drago and generals have been lost. Major Guido Verona informs that Major General Drago died in Casteltermini.

With family dowries, the death of parents and siblings causes deep shock to the citizens and the mayor's office of Montemaggiore Belsito and Militello. Life is tragic. The easy life and optimism disappear from the wheel of illusion, which charges vertiginous. The Supreme Being is the ultimate creator. Everything is possible in the end. Great mysteries scattered through life, among tombs and chambers. The memory of the dead burn and illuminate our grand opera. Carducci for the dead.

9

CORONEL DOCTOR
EMILIO MILITELLO

He graduated in medicine in Naples, entered the military career and in 1917 obtained the rank of lieutenant colonel. He was in the African campaign in 1895 and 96, as well as in the Far East in 1912 and in expeditions in 1911. In the last war he suffered an illness that caused him to rest in the military reserve. During the war he was awarded the Knight's Cross in the Order of the S.S.M. of the Crown of Italy. He died on January 11, 1945.

10

MONSIGNOR DOCTOR RAFAELE ARRIGO

Laureate theologian and lawyer at the Athenaeum, Roman Seminary in 1901. Professor of Theology at the Seminary of Patti and then in Cefalù. Archpriest of Montemaggiore, his native town. In 1904 he was appointed abbot of St. Mary of the Angels. He founded the house of St. Angela de la Monca Orbolano and the teacher Pia Filippina. He renovated the parish house and the people remember that he wrote a volume called Senador Animarum: the life of Monsignor M. M. Teresi Davide. 1932, Florence, the beatifications of Teresi.

11

MONTEMAGGIORE MEDALLIONS

Many men rush in the fleeting resistance that causes a sunset. Much sadness, the men of misery. The man who has an impulse, though he informs his fellows without survival. Many are wrong in his life. In Montemaggiore there are men who live of ancestors, live of sacrifice, of honor and glory. Without lesser nothing, some people testify to be living in tranquility.

PROFESSOR MEDICAL DOCTOR CAPTAIN GIUSEPPE MENDOLA

He became a doctor at the University of Palermo. In his military career he was a captain in the Navy. He studied at the best teaching university of special surgical pathologies, University of Rome.

13

PROFESSOR FRANCESCO BIONDOLILLO

With a great scientific literary profession, was in controversy the procurator Francesco Biondolillo. In the Italian literary proposal he then experimented in the field of poetry. Journalist in the volume of the poets, he is critical composer. Next to every study in the publications Macarronea of Martin Corai.

Spinello Verticone talks about Biondolillo in the Italian newspaper on September 16, 1981. The spiritual unity of The Divine Comedy, History of Literature and Gothic Italian aesthetics, await publication. In 1923 he teaches Italian literature with the qualifications of the exam at the R. University of Palermo and the high literary university work in Rome. Biondolillo was a complete man, very severe in studies, father in word and family.

14

DOCTOR PROFESSOR PIETRO DRAGO

Man of culture and philosopher, illuminating the reality of 21 year olds in Palermo. He studied philosophy and literature. His mission was to preside the gymnasium of Cagli in Montemaggiore. He was a professor at the scientific Lyceum of Perugia and teacher at the university. He published The Kantian mysticism; Messina house with the G. principality in 1929; The notes to Berg, poet in 1930; Concrete ethics of Bologna and Emiliano in 1932; Genesis of the phenomenological problem, Milano Editors principality in 1933; Hebbel, Rome Editors A. F. Formigoni; Immortality and survival, international philosopher, Logos Napoli in 1933; The Sicily in 1945; E. L. L. L. Libera Italiana Editions.

Another volume for the stamp, with many reviews and appreciations of the best studies of today. Read Italian magazines, the latest publications. The judge reads from the messenger Padano on November 16, 1933 a long article on the interpretations of Habbel. Pietro Drago says that he has come to revive the artistic human drama.

Federico Habbel was a great representative of modern culture. The Habbelian productions, with sympathetic instructions of the fulfilled argument, made Drago raise a very important profile. That was what was necessary. The German grammarian's hard mood was the energetic impulse for the literary periodical *Buadrifio* of Rome.

On November 15, 1933, *Palermo Literary Today* joined the library and the philosophy of Dr. Amato, tireless of the beautiful lecture hall in memory of the communications of Pietro Drago. The dynamic writing of thirty years, philosopher of high level, works like a glove for the Italian scholar S. E. G. Marconi. On April 21, 1934 he celebrates the birth of Rome.

On November 5, 1933, the Mussolini Awards are attended by H.M. the King. 1662 academic, foreign and professional competitors. Pietro Strada, Palermo philosophical publications for 2,000 lire, see newspaper of the night messenger.

April 24, 1934, People of Rome, Sicilian newspaper. Then the Academy of Italy makes the pledge to the King Emperor of the *Duce*, winning the prize of L50,000 Pietro Drago, in Palermo.

La Stampa newspaper, April 22nd, 1942. According to the Italian newspaper, Drago has the best brains and traditions of Renaissance Palermo.

Spinoza, February 11, 1929, Giordano Bruno. Fasc III fuestran-cello of goat VII, Civil Review of Roberto Ruggiero. The civil institutions in Messina, 1930. The new Italy. History of religions. November 12, 1930, philosophy, the right of Africans. 1932, Modern History of Florence, National Reviews, Federico Habbel. The vandalism, Rome 1338.

On March 28, 1935 he took a splendid examination at the University of Rome and graduated. In 1947 he began teaching philosophy to young people at the University of Turin and then in Rome. We got him in the Government missions, in the area of propaganda of Italian culture for two years. The propaganda of the diplomatic intellectual missions, the illustrations of our homeland, with much appreciation to the great homeland. Sicily is very cultural and there are many Italian newspapers that want activity in Italy.

Leer Handela Ochg, February 20, 1948. Uppsala Uga Tidning Onsdagen, February 25, 1948. Goteborg Morganpos, February 20, 1947. The European, November 7, 1948.

15

PRIEST LAWYER EMILIO DRAGO

Our dear friend Emilio Drago, a cultured young man with a religious profile, has the courage to do missionary work in the great ranks, at God's side. Encouraged as a religious by the service to the Lord to his relatives. He is a Jesuit with studies, happy and with the best aspirations. The newspaper, December 10, 1932.

The youth of Rome, October 23, 1932. The young lawyers that the Lord calls them to the last war, the faithful fighters of the regiment. World War II, two war criminals and fighters from the ruins. The involvement of large families help the dead, wounded and dying. The chaplain had to walk and more if they were angry.

The fighters gave him the name of Colonel commander of the X regiment of the *bersaglieri*. The officers left the prison of the State, said by the officer of the regiment in Africa in seven nations. You are put to the admiration all of you of Ain

Gazala. The best of the military of the regiment are finished as fighters.

Always on the side of the battle, helping everyone, he seeks recognition on the battlefield. He was imprisoned in Agedabia, with the fate of the others, first to Salluk and then in Benghazi. He preached the good of all in Benghazi, in the concentration camp with the troops. He obtained permission to move from the English authorities and changed the food to the prisoners, because in the early days they were not given food by the military of the regiment. When they went elsewhere, he continued the assistance to alleviate the pain. They hid in Gebel with several *bersaglieri* released by the troops. He returned to the regiment for assistance of spiritual morale to the military of the presidium in Agedabia.

16

MONSIGNOR DOCTOR LIBORIO SCACCIA

He was born in Montemaggiore Belsito on July 26, 1910. He studied at the Pontifical Roman Seminary in Rome and was ordained a priest in 1933. He graduated in Economic Law with high marks in culture and worked for the Holy See as secretary and auditor in Bolivia, Uruguay, Argentina and Paraguay.

After nine years, in 1948 he was appointed Secretary of State with diplomatic missions. In his village Montemaggiore, he is a manifest citizen in all actions of a society-forming nature. The greatest adventure of a people with wealth, with all the honors, is the pride of a civil and prosperous people.

Noble in character, possessive, intelligent and prepared for culture, he feels proud and satisfied to give to a misunderstood mass. Thus, thinking people, educated professionals and intellectuals leave the village. Meanwhile, at the foot of the hills, people plant vegetables. They still see cases and hope that the animal world will be transformed.

There are four brotherly and religious towns, which make solemn celebrations to the deceased. Religious, human and civil sentiments help the fellowship, as well as the beaten work of the old. It is necessary to limit the service of the unhappy and wicked.

Montemaggiore Belsito, with an area of 2,064 hectares and a population of 7,500 inhabitants, has no relations with other border territories. Caccamo Aliminusa of Sclafani has 1,072 inhabitants on 13,506 hectares for the year 1944. It is necessary the feeling of justice and civility in common with other towns, even those municipalities that are only a few centuries old. A microscopic territory, the municipality of Antonino Militello in 1925, is distinguished by its culture, justice and patriotism, supported by the good government of the King.

In 1928, the territorial districts were extended with the proper documentation, because the citizens expected justice from Militello's illustrious force. The circle of Belsito is closed. He was recognized in Montemaggiore for his merits as an illustrious man that history remembers, surpassing Termine.

Alia remembers Dr. Cardinale, in the company of God, professor of Greek, Latin and Italian Literature, and H. E. Dr. T. Guccione, professor of Pathological Anatomy at the University of Sassari. Aliminusa and Milone are also recognized as courageous jurists. Caccamo highlights Lafate in

Faso, philosopher and biologist, as well as the illustrious Professor Addo.

According to Giuffré, a professor at the University of Palermo, other countries live without memories. In these small towns we remember him, loving him for the past, for the present and the future. The cult of memory is not only affection, it is a duty, it is love of country with warlike sentiment. We citizens should not be ashamed.

17

THE OFFENDER'S CHILDREN
(HISTORICAL ROMANCE)

Every man and woman have their romances. The newspaper closes the grave, cruel tears in the silence, the cruel of publicity. No thoughts, no pity of loves, of compassion. Life from pain to tragedies, dramas without solutions and without cries ignored in silence. The known metastasis has to be tried, that for life shines.

See it and follow it, a sun star, a sincere compass. Virtue at the sacrifice of the darkness of the past. A romance that shows that man's love obfuscates mind, heart and soul. Man's duty, in delirium yields to Plegan man. Evil has to do its duty.

The first meeting. The day died in the district of Sicily, a purple red inflamed the top of the world. The calm sky, in the air throbbed dark prayer of hope, with the silence and the melody of the church bells. They arrived in campaign, invite to prayer and call the poet. The love that binds us to life, that feels pain and sadness, happiness and melody. The door of the unknown and sadness, the agony to the light.

The face is troubled. Luigi is thinking, with eyes to the sky and sighs. My question, plus worries and thoughts, How many sad worries! Bad omen of the past.

Do not speak ill of our country, of beautiful Italy. Love for my homeland, it would be a crime to speak ill of the homeland. The grave is our death, the lack of immense love. In the chest does not weigh the heart and life is a pang of melancholy, it is like a funeral lamp.

Mattiucho must believe me. I cannot go near the country and I am heartbroken by this trip, in return for this barbaric war. In infamy weighs the judgment of God.

Luigi is silent as the sky lights up.

- «Whip the horse,» Matthew says and threatens him, accompanied by thunder, blood and rain.

A horse shelter is needed in the town of Alia. In the paper are civility, threats and cruel relatives, flattery, truce, assassins, torture, travel, campaigning and meeting the Lord.

My father was a fellow citizen of this country. He had an unhappy name and the last word you know is the bad fortune of your family. Forgive me, young man, for ill fortune knocked at your door. You know the rich, you don't know God. They are evildoers. I claim the honor of my parents, for you are young and can reach the goals in the spring of years.

I can hear the voice of the confused youth and I am filled with tears for my unhappy life.

A girl dressed in white appeared at the door, looking divine, with deep eyes and soft beauty. Luigi was astonished. She was the death and life of his passions. The two young men rise respectfully with deep reverence. They are children of family adventures. Gentlemen, the word is beautiful and dear, adventure and panache.

Luigi did not know how to answer. He remembered the hope of life and the young people thanked the old man with much hospitality. In a room, some flowers of life and a deep bow. Anna said:

- «Give the flowers to the unhappy young men, who want passions for silence. The promises of love are gone.»

Luigi arrived, gave the last good look at the girl in his eyes. Below, Matteo's heart full of sarcasm, silent when he sees the girl, only the deep black eyes. It reads all black soul and a magic in the heart.

I love you. Still on the last Sunday of carnival the sky was filled with stars, because I will love with the depths of my soul, without ceasing. From a deep mouth, the water of the fountain pronounces a name. It prefers a dream name: Luigi. Incessantly on the lips, the pathetic moon suffers in silence, beautiful.

Slowly, looking at the moon, the rays of sunlight enter from the window. She puts her hand to her chest, the suicide of the Gioconda, the poor girl with the black eyes abandons herself in an armchair. Anna says to him:

- «Why are you always alone? Mother, I need your comfort, your advice, your help.»

Being the mother, she embraces her children with emotion.

- "Anna, my daughter, how much I love you!»

The mother never spoke like that and the girl abandons herself to her mother with a tight embrace to her heart and a face full of tears.

- «Mother, I'm unhappy, I'm sad,» she exclaims.

- «Speak, daughter, speak,» she says kissing her head.

- «Last spring we were fine. Today it's a raging hurricane that goes berserk and set to be hospitalized. In the evening, dressed up, everything is fine. I heard it the first time, narrating the steps to my father.»

- How, my daughter, did you hide all this from me that night? Why didn't you tell me? Give up hope and turn to yourself to that man, your love, who will make you happy.»

- «Mother of God...»

- «Forget that hapless man, my pain, his words and his appearance. That man never loved you. He did not appear to all eyes. Poor child, you have to resign yourself. Remember that your cousin Giacomo loves you madly and can make you happy.»

- «He loves me, but I don't love him and at the third turn I feel it in my ears. Giacomo is rich, but I don't want his wealth.»

- «Don't call him, daughter. Speak because he lives, imagine. Enthusiasm is indispensable in the young, like the beauty that adorns the heart,» thus speaks the pained mother.

The room, the illuminated piano, the carnival in the largest room of Doctor Guccione, brave music teacher. In the immense party, a little girl in love sitting in a corner. Her roses, her saddened lips and a wise and mysterious sigh.

- «You are the queen of the party. With this dance I feel that I am happy.»

The boy sits next to the girl. He is a young man of thirty, short and thick, dark-skinned, rough and vulgar in all his movements. He approaches the young woman and says:

- «You are the queen of the party. I prepared the dance at home, thinking of your happiness. You are beautiful.»

Away from the party, this was fire burning in the girl's spirits. The cousin tells her:

- «Vil! Don't insult my spirits.»

Painting and sculpture, costumes of taste and beauty. He approaches the piano and begins to play extensively alone the notes of Berlin. That year, for all the masks he does not go to his place. He puts on a green ribbon and sings, to great applause. Only Anna does not bat her hands. In front of the mask she looks moved and restless, as when the two hearts meet.

Luigi removes his mask.

- «I do know you,» the girl says. - «I want to say a lot of things, although I'd like to talk too.»

Luigi puts on his mask and takes advantage of it and approaches Anna, saying in her ear:

- «Sweet dove, girl. The flowers of my life, the first kiss».

The night was dark and Luigi, wrapped in a cloak, goes to Anna's house, watching from afar those games in the square with big steps. The girl was the consoling angel. Anna, Luigi, the two names were pronounced with a whisper. She goes to a stable, where she gets an oil lamp, a table and several things to ride. Says the young man of her beloved:

- «Anna, soul of my heart, I am the happiest. When you first saw me, I was unhappy thinking you rejected me. I love you,» he tells her. - It is not martyrdom or torment, but the other night I did not feel you. I live a bad torment in our heart. My Mother, I stay close to you.»

- «Your mother is not sick, she's fine now.»

- Mom is wrinkled and her hair is disheveled. My mother is a good lady, not a great frivolous lady. She is a good lady, full of affection and greatness. The battle goes on, life, the horizon of my youth,» so spoke Luigi.

A lot of heat, a single roof, a sigh. The father figure would console the pains and sadness. That is my dream, my hope of youth. The old man visits the horses and goes back to sleep. With the presence of seeing each other again tomorrow, the two loves look at each other with passion and give each other their first kiss. Luigi is in the street. Anna watches until he disappears and walks away quickly.

Luigi is sitting at the table, reading the work of Mazzini Eugenio, his dearest friend. With the newspaper in hand, Eugenio says «Poor Italy - what a shame!. The dear soul and many victims. Luigi takes the newspaper from Sicily and reads several telegrams. The homeland, the siege is imposed. We were martyrs. Italy ignores the lack of confessions. Italy's song, «Capitolio», which spoils Cartaginense. In the world, the fairs that bend the knees.

Facing the Romans, with many enemies and difficult places, I can die the life that the Italians gave me. In Europe, the Greeks walked glorious, 300 cadets at Thermopylae. Italy remembers the brave dead at Novare and Solferino, at San Quintino. Napoleon called brave his soldiers who died with weapons in hand, from the pyramids of Russia and France. Then the great problem of Caesar and Pompeii. The valiant dead in Novara, the Galiani, are thousands and thousands of dead in the fight, with the songs of Italy on their lips.

Luigi saw the letter with his address. How happy I felt! Nearby, the incessant thought, the soprano of my heart. «Luigi you are gone. Luigi, you departed and left me the memory, the love. The comfort of my heart is in the cold earth, in the sun that warms you, in the cold that hits you. You left me alone with the images in my heart. When will we meet again, my love? I have many things to tell you.»

Luigi reads the pages, professing: Beautiful creature. She loves me with feeling. My heart beats with love, being fire and flame in my heart. Now think to answer me. Read and reread, love. The stretch to Caesar, the future in God's hands, the eyes to see the heart, to call the very distant sight.

«The delinquent's son loves me,» Anna says squeezing her hands, without permission. «Luigi, I love you very much. Even though I love you, already daddy and mommy are engaged to be married and you come back late. Luigi, I dedicate a prayer to you. Goods are the fruit of delight when I remember the piano.»

Now the girl starts playing the piano with great ease. Luigi watches with passion. He no longer lived in that world, Dante's seventh heaven. He places a kiss on her cheek and Anna blushes, smiling. «I feel happy, I am embraced by my prayers,"Luigi says. «The letter I wrote had many things to say to you, my love.

Luigi says to the girl:

- «Run! Dad is coming. Save yourself! I see no other way out, it will have been worth the sacrifice.»

At that moment she puts him in a dressing room. Anna runs into the rooms.

- «I don't see another life,» the girl says.

She doesn't know and is chained by the arm. Luigi takes her to the dressing room and tells her:

- «You must hide. Keep the key.»

Anna advances in space. She had made a crime and died, did not know how to receive the uncles. The music invited her, the affection, the hidden guest, the son possessed the girl, who is frightened with feeling.

- «Dad, what do you say!« she exclaims.

- «What an inexperienced girl who does not know life! We are murderers of the family, relatives of thieves and criminals, inhabitants of Montemaggiore.»

Banditry announces the victim of death if it is under the pandoro vase. Land of death, announcement of the victim.

Anna is naive. Lots of flattery, listens for a long time and gets thousands. She does not know the authority of the father. Anna, your father's words, busy and breathless. The tempest of the heart, the prayer, the mother alone, the husband, the ears that hold the sigh. He secures the bed. He appears agitated, with eyes to the face with pity.

18

NEWSPAPERS AND BOOKS

ll the newspapers in Italy against the magistrates:

-*El sole*, December 3, 1901, December 21, 1901, February 1902, March 9, 1902.

-*Il periodico di Sicilia*, August 6, 1902, September 2, 1903, October 6, 1903, February 12, 1094, August 27, 1903, May 16, 1901.

-*The Tribune*, September 4, 1903.

-*Il secolo Milano*, September 3, 1903, September 9, 1903, September 20, 1903.

-*La bataglia*, September 13, 1903.

-*La torbice*, September 24, 1903, October 4, 1903.

-*Resto del quartino*, September 10, 1903.

-*La Difesa*, February 7, 1904.

-*Domenica del corriere*, September 20, 1900, January 2, 1936.

The major force that suffocates goes completely in the dark. A people, the unhappy victim. Returned greeting of human solidarity having affection.

-Carlino, September 10, 1903.

Civil offender for saving himself from a long sentence. On the guilty, with eyes to heaven, bitter remorse and unhappy for life.

Military and civilian banditry in Sicily. The truth is yet to be known. Don Pepino kidnaps victims of the gang. He condemns Biagio Valvo, leader of the gang. The soldiers on horseback, maintained by the government of the day and the mafia of the authority in contention. The prefect. Death of Valvo, all under arrest.

ABOUT THE AUTHOR

Teresa Di Sclafani De Nasca was born in Italy. She has also lived in Venezuela and the United States.

MORE WORKS BY TERESA DI SCLAFANI DE NASCA

-*The world according to Teresa Di Sclafani*

-*The Diary of Teresa Di Sclafani*

Each one is available in Castilian («Spanish»), English and Tuscan (standard Italian).

www.ingramcontent.com/pod-product-compliance
Lightning Source LLC
Chambersburg PA
CBHW051645120626
46551CB00015B/2231